The Baseball Short Story Anthology

Other Titles By Connie Ragen Green

Living the Mentored Life

Rethinking the Work Ethic: Embrace the Struggle and Exceed Your Own Potential

Doing What It Takes: The Online Entrepreneur's Playbook

Book. Blog. Broadcast. – The Trifecta of Entrepreneurial Success

Write Publish Prosper: How to Write Prolifically, Publish Globally, and Prosper Eternally

The Transformational Entrepreneur: Creating a Life of Dedication and Service

Living the Internet Lifestyle: Quit Your Job, Become an Entrepreneur, and Live Your Ideal Life

The Inner Game of Internet Marketing

The Weekend Marketer: Say Goodbye to the "9 to 5", Build an Online Business, and Live the Life You Love

What is Your Why?

Time Management Strategies for Entrepreneurs: How to Manage Your Time to Increase Your Bottom Line

Huge Profits with Affiliate Marketing: How to Build an Online Empire by Recommending What You Love

Membership Sites Made Simple

Article Marketing: How to Attract New Prospects, Create Products, and Increase Your Income

Targeted Traffic Techniques

Other Titles By Connie Ragen Green, Continued

Huge Profits With a Tiny List: 50 Ways to Use Relationship Marketing to Increase Your Bottom Line

The Baseball Short Story Anthology

By
Connie Ragen Green

Copyright © 2018 by Hunter's Moon Publishing

ISBN Paperback: 978-1-937988-37-1

ISBN Kindle: 978-1-937988-38-8

Hunter's Moon Publishing
http://HuntersMoonPublishing.com

Interior Design by Shawn Hansen
Cover Design by Shawn Hansen

Dedication

To all baseball fans, whoever you are, wherever you live, and whichever team you follow. As you make the commitment to be there for your team, through ups and downs, trials and tribulations, broadcasting schedules, injuries, and inclement weather delays, know that you are appreciated by the other fans, the players, and everyone it takes to make the world of baseball carry on over the decades and into the future.

And to the kids who are in the process of becoming lifelong fans, know that you are observing history in the making. Someday you'll be telling stories and sharing memories with your own children, just as the adults in your life are sharing with you right now. Learn from baseball as you would from school; everything you need to know about math, science, social studies, and most importantly, about people and the relationships between them can be learned from watching and playing baseball. And if you take these lessons to heart your life will be everything you are dreaming of, and so much more.

DEDICATION

Table of Contents

Pre-Game

Baseball Short Stories came about as a result of a renewed friendship with a man I knew during the 1980s while he was living in the Los Angeles area. We had lost track of each other over the past three decades and were able to reconnect after a few searches on the internet. During one of our early phone conversations right after the first of the year in 2018, he asked me if I remembered going to a baseball game with him in 1985 between the Los Angeles Angels and the Toronto Blue Jays. I was sorry to have to tell him that I could not remember going to the game on that day so long ago.

We then went on to talk about baseball and that's when I realized that he was a true fan, having been a part of this magical world since he was a small boy, playing the game and watching with family members and friends, and continuing to watch or attend as many games as possible up through the present day. I found myself becoming enthralled with his stories about his favorite team and of baseball in general and thought back to how baseball had played a part in my own life over the years.

After some thought I announced to him at the beginning of March that I was committed to watching as many games as possible when the new season began at the end of that month. I'm sure my friend thought at the time it was a nice gesture, but that I would most likely grow weary of watching and discussing baseball within the first month or so.

But I am a person of my word, and in the process of carving out time in my already extremely busy schedule I fell in love with the game of baseball, and in particular with my new favorite team, the New York Yankees.

There is so much to know, and over the months as the new season unfolded my friend and I spoke often so he could answer my seemingly endless questions, share stories with me related to the players and the teams over the years, and educate me about things that were confusing.

It turned out that I knew even less about baseball than I thought I did. When did pitchers start throwing so many different kinds of balls? Why did the roster change from week to week? And why did foul balls count as strikes sometimes and not count at all at others? And why did every player on every team carry around their own personal bats?

When I emailed him a laundry list of my questions he would politely decline to answer in that way, preferring to speak on the phone so we could interact instead of just trading information in writing. Soon I was getting up to speed and even knew which teams were in the American League and which were in the National League. I told him that no one in my life had ever been willing to take the time or had the patience to teach me about baseball and thanked him for doing so with me.

At some point during early May I came up with this idea of putting together an anthology of short stories related to baseball. I ran the idea past my friend and he said he had a story or two he could possibly share. It was obvious that his enthusiasm for this project was guarded at first, while mine was over the top. But I am persistent when I have an idea, and will do almost anything to complete a project that I believe will be of benefit to so many people.

If you love baseball, you will enjoy reading these stories. If baseball has touched your life in any way over the years, you may find yourself within these pages. And if you find yourself thinking about baseball while you are doing something else far removed from the ball field, perhaps you will agree that this is a magical game that has become the fabric of many of our lives.

Connie Ragen Green
Author & Editor

Top of the First

Baseball is one of those things that make you take a closer look at yourself and ask the tough questions about who you have become as a human being. Questions like:

Would I have the grit and discipline to go out for a professional sport?

When the going got tough, would I be willing to do what it takes to stay in the game?

Would I be able to compartmentalize my life in order to have the mental toughness to excel?

How would I handle the relationships between the players, the management, the coaches, and the fans?

Could anything in my life be as important as baseball is to the top players?

In those answers I found the strength to forgive myself for dreams not realized and for opportunities not taken. Baseball is now a permanent part of my life story and I am on my way to becoming a better person because of it.

I hope that you enjoy each of these stories, as well as the poems. They are all true and written from the hearts of this anthology's authors. Onward now to stories from the fields of dreams...

First Inning

Connie Ragen Green

Softball and Success:
How Sports Can Change Your Life

While I was a classroom teacher I was always looking for opportunities to make my students feel successful. Many times this occurred as a result of something I presented to them as a challenge, and out of just pure fun for everyone. Softball came under this category and it was one of the best confidence building activities we ever got involved with as a class.

For many years I taught fifth and sixth grade students. My kids were from the inner city of Los Angeles and few had any experiences with team sports away from school. During the first week of classes we would go outside for physical education (P.E.) in the afternoon and we would play softball as a class, with half of us on one side and half on the other. What they didn't know, unless they had older siblings or friends who had told them in advance, was that my class softball teams were legendary at the school where I was teaching.

During that first week I was looking for two things. First, I needed a pitcher. Like I mentioned, few of my kids had played in Little League or any other organized team away from school, so I was hoping for some raw talent to emerge and was never disappointed. My motto was "If I have one decent pitcher it will be a good school year; if I have two pitchers the school year will be fantastic."

The second thing I was looking for was confidence in my players. The rule was that everyone had to take a turn at bat, boys and girls alike. As each child approached home plate I was searching for something in their demeanor that would show me they had confidence in their ability to be a part of our team and strive to improve their skills. I loved watching the kids help each other with this process - how to stand, where to stand, how to hold the bat, how to keep your eye on the ball, and so forth.

The helpers in this case were the natural leaders, and those who were willing to be coached were those with the greatest potential. And while we were practicing during this first week of school and into the next few weeks everyone got to hit the ball, no matter how many pitches it took. This required my pitchers to make adjustments to better serve the batter. They had to move in closer sometimes, especially for the girls who had typically never come this close to a bat or a softball. They also adjusted their pitches, something that would serve them well later on when we were playing more seasoned players. And when someone was reluctant to take their turn at bat I would plead with them to give it a try. "When you finally hit that ball it will be the best feeling in the world!" I would exclaim, and when they did they knew for themselves that I had not been exaggerating one bit.

And the level of confidence that came about from playing this sport amazed even me. Some of my most timid girls and boys, children who had never spoken up for themselves in the past seemed to come alive when they were successful on the softball field. I was so proud of them and knew they had a much better chance at lifelong success because of their experiences during this time.

Playing softball was the highlight of being in school for many of the students all year long. Yes, we played from the time school began until the last day of the school year and many of my students became quite good during this time. But before I share that part of the story, allow me to tell you what happened after that first month of practice with only my class involved. That is when I would casually say to one of the other fifth or sixth grade teachers, preferably in front of their classes as we were coming or going to recess or lunch "would your class like to play against my class in a softball game?" Of course they wanted to and the match was on!

Even though over the years everyone in the school knew this day was coming, I was amazed that not one of the other teachers ever practiced with their kids during the first month we were there. It was awesome to see all of my kids confidently taking their place on the field or in the batting lineup during our challenges with the other classes. Usually a few of my kids had a glove, and over the years I collected more gloves, a few bats, and even a catcher's mask to contribute to the cause.

The other classes were pleasantly surprised when we shared these gloves and other equipment with them, whether they were in the field or up at bat. And if one of their players had not ever hit a baseball, one or two of my kids would rush forward to assist them with their stance and their positioning of hands on the bat. This was a beautiful thing to see, and because I always wear my sunglasses when I'm outdoors no one could see the occasional tear fall down my cheek.

I have to say that playing softball each year with my class was the best thing I ever did as a teacher to help my students achieve more, in the classroom and beyond the classroom. And some of the kids went on to play baseball in junior high and high school, something they might not have done otherwise. Teamwork, being present with your classmates, and focusing on something that is so special and important made for kids who were more likely to see the "big picture" of their life. If you can face down a pitcher who is a foot taller, more experienced, and hungry for a win and still hit a single, you can achieve most anything in your life.

Part of the Team

Connie Ragen Green

During the mid 1980s I worked as a production assistant for a large film and animation production company in Los Angeles. It was a magical time in my life where I had left the world of academia and was finding myself by exploring alternative possibilities for jobs and a career path. The production company was filled with people and ideas that I was not familiar with and soon I became immersed in the culture of big Hollywood productions. I was hired as a production assistant, which meant that I ran errands and did odd jobs that were not a part of anyone else's job description.

Sometimes I drove to LAX to pick up someone arriving from France or Japan, the two international locations of this company. And this is where I first used a fax machine, back when it was called a "facsimile" and required you to stand next to the machine (a huge one) and wait until the paper you had sent had gone through successfully. This took several minutes and it was deemed a success when the paper came out the other side with a small red line printed on the page. Then you placed a phone call to the person overseas who was to receive this document and waited for them to acknowledge receipt of it in a form that could be read correctly on their end. And the pay was better than I had ever received during my working career. Yes, these were the good old days.

But the most magical part of this experience occurred when I was invited to join the company's baseball team. I asked if they meant softball, but was informed immediately that this was baseball. Yes, I wanted to play and curbed my enthusiasm lest they think I had an ulterior motive of some kind. This was Hollywood, after all.

I showed up at the park a few minutes shy of the appointed time, wearing jeans and a tee shirt and a baseball cap. When they saw I had a glove and the appropriate shoes for playing they welcomed me onto the field. That's when I looked up into the bleachers and saw the other employees, both male and female, who were wearing clothes more suited to business and definitely not the correct foot attire for baseball.

I had played softball a little over the course of my lifetime, but never baseball. And I had never been a real athlete although I did enjoy the outdoors and relished the idea of being a part of it all. One of the staff writers tossed me a ball and I caught it easily. He smiled and I knew they would let me play if I could earn my keep.

The opposing team showed up soon after. These players were from another production company in Los Angeles and looked like they meant business. They wore matching maroon tee shirts and had some serious equipment with them. They did not smile or even make eye contact, and soon the game began.

I don't remember the score or even if my team won or lost that day. But I do remember hitting the ball and running to first base and the way that made me feel. I was a part of this group and had value as a team member. At some point the game was over and I was included in their ritual of going to a local pub for beer and sandwiches. I sat on an end seat and ordered a hot dog and a lemonade and thought about how lucky I was to be there on that day.

Many games followed, and during my three month stint as a production assistant I witnessed many experiences on the baseball field that helped mold me into the person I wanted to be. There was a combination of sportsmanship, mentorship, and fellowship I had not been a part of during my life up to that point. And that's when I first pitched a story idea out loud. It was to J. Michael Straczynski (we called him Joe), the head writer and story editor at that time and someone who is still going strong as a force in the world of science fiction and may be best known for his work on Babylon 5. I'll never forget the advice he gave me; he told me not to talk about my story ideas but to write them down. "I want to read your story, not hear about it," he said with great wisdom.

My goal in taking the job at the production company was to explore some possibilities for my future. I have to say this was a golden opportunity for me in many ways as I was able to connect with people who were unlike any I had ever met in the past. And even though I was warned against spending too much time with a post-production group because of their union regulations, I still got to see more than I ever thought I would.

And the people who visited regularly were of great interest as well. Michael Jackson stopped by a few times to see a young woman who worked in the art department. She told me later that she accompanied him on set and to public functions at times because he did not like to be left alone.

And one of the producers had a poster on her wall of a woman she had met in Chicago before moving to Los Angeles earlier that year to work with this company. She told me this woman was destined for great things and that I should remember her name. I did. It was Oprah Winfrey. And when the head of the company asked me to drive into Los Angeles one night to deliver a script to someone, I did so enthusiastically and with professionalism without giving any thought to who it might be. It was science fiction author and screenwriter Ray Bradbury (Fahrenheit 451), who was in the midst of producing The Ray Bradbury Theater. He didn't drive and had things delivered to his front door regularly. We spoke for a few minutes, and now I regret not coming inside to have a cup of coffee with him after he graciously asked me to one time. I also delivered scripts to Harlan Ellison, who was at that time working on a screenplay that ended up in litigation with another production company and a large film studio.

These experiences helped shape my thinking and my life, and it all came back to the baseball team for me. It was on the field where my deepest friendships grew and I was able to observe and ask questions. I played my best, kept a low profile, and learned more about who I was and what I wanted from my life in the future than I had during college or graduate school or while working at any jobs I had been at previously.

The Baseball Letters

Connie Ragen Green

The year was 1977 and I was living in New York City. Having graduated from UCLA in June, I was now attending law school on the opposite coast and in a whole new world. My husband had taken a job in the Middle East as a way to earn more income than he could in the States. As a general contractor he was in high demand by international companies, and the job he was placed on was with the Ralph M. Parsons Company building an air strip for the government in Riyadh, Saudi Arabia.

These were the days when you called the operator if you wanted to make an overseas call. They would attempt to connect you, but many times the lines were at capacity and they would ring you back when the line was available. The calls were expensive but necessary. The only other communication we had was through the hand written letters we wrote to each other every week.

Summer turned into fall and the weather changed so quickly it caught me off guard. Having lived in southern California for most of my life I was accustomed to a kinder, gentler change of season. My law school studies were tedious and required me to work twelve hours a day in order to catch up with my peers each day. I needed a way to relax and unwind and when the New York Yankees looked like they would be in the World Series that year against the Los Angeles Dodgers it was the perfect way to spend my precious leisure time in my little apartment in the Sutton Place neighborhood of the city.

My husband also loved baseball, so my letters became a play by play of each game leading up to and including the World Series. I would take copious notes during each inning of every game and then write them up as a "play by play" recap in my letters to him. Soon I heard that these letters were being shared with other American workers in his area so they could also experience the details of what happened and imagine they were actually at the game.

Reggie Jackson had already been dubbed "Mr. October" by teammate Mickey Munson, so it made sense for me to highlight him in each letter I prepared that month. Day by day and game by game, I chronicled the history of baseball from in front of my television set in Manhattan so that many others would be kept abreast of what was happening back in America. The Yankees won the World Series on October 18th at Yankee Stadium. It was game 6 of the series and lasted for two hours and eighteen minutes. There were 56,497 fans in attendance and the cheers circled the globe.

Looking back, it is difficult to imagine that we lived in such a distant world back in 1977. These days people everywhere can experience things large and small simultaneously. But perhaps there was a joy back then in not knowing until much later what was happening in your part of the world if you were away. I do know that baseball in general and the World Series more specifically drew my husband and I closer together while he was so far away. When he returned just after Christmas he spilled out his cardboard box of letters on to the kitchen table and I understood at once what they had meant to him.

Tattered and dog-eared, each letter had been read over and over and passed from one person to another. For a moment I was self-conscious about any spelling or grammatical mistakes I had made, but that quickly dissipated as I saw the tears of joy in his eyes. My letters about baseball had kept him connected to his homeland during months of uncertainty and loneliness. And knowing that I had taken the time to include each play as thoroughly as possible during this time was seen by him as my outpouring of love and respect for him and the game he loved so much.

Four years later my husband passed away after fifteen months of battling leukemia. He had gone on another overseas work assignment the year before, and when he returned to the States he went to Memorial Sloan-Kettering hospital in mid-town Manhattan for treatment. It was there that I last saw him and where he thanked me for the "baseball letters" of several years before. It was interesting to me that even though we both lived in California we were now sitting in a hospital room just over a mile away from where I had lived in that tiny apartment on Second Avenue and Fifty-first Street in Manhattan and less than eight miles from Yankee Stadium in the Bronx. That apartment was where I had watched the games and reported the outcomes to him and his fellow workers by taking copious notes and turning them into my "baseball letters" to share with all of them.

Life is always surprising me with its coincidences, which I believe are not coincidences at all. The Yankees helped me to stay connected with the most important person in my life at that time in a way that few things can. And I will never forget those hours of sitting in front of that small television screen and recording events that are forever a part of our American history.

"Randy, Randy, Randy!"

Connie Ragen Green

When the social worker popped open the trunk of her car the rancid smell jumped out at me quickly. There were several large garbage bags filled with clothing for a very small boy, so it was a surprise when the boy who eventually emerged from the back seat was much bigger than I expected. He didn't make eye contact at first so I went back to the trunk to see what lay beneath the bags of smelly clothes.

It was a bicycle, again too small for the boy now standing in front of me. There was a story here that I would eventually know but was not quite ready to hear.

She encouraged him to say hello to me and when our eyes met I saw both strength and a sadness that was haunting. He extended his little arm to shake my hand and at that moment I wanted to wrap my arms around him and promise him that I would make it all better and protect him from the evils of the world. But instead, I maintained my composure and said,

"Hi Randy. I'm Connie. I'm glad you're here."

The social worker did give Randy a little hug and then drove slowly around the cul-de-sac and onto the main road as we watched her shiny white Buick get smaller and smaller and then finally disappear.

~*~*~

I had wanted to become a foster parent because I honestly believed that it was my calling to do so. I wanted to provide a safe

14

environment for one or two children who were in the middle of a life they had not chosen and who needed to understand that most people were basically good. Little did I know that I would become involved in a situation where so much had happened to a five year old boy that was horrific in nature.

Randy and I bonded quickly and that was due in part to the help of Mickey, my little Yorkie. She quickly became Randy's best friend and was the first living creature to love him unconditionally. During our first days together they were inseparable and Randy spent time on Monday morning explaining why he was leaving her behind to go to school. It was a beautiful moment I will never forget.

As much as I could offer Randy at home, I knew that he needed more. I wanted him to have friends his own age, to be surrounded by caring adults, and to experience the value of team work. There was only one answer in my mind, and that was baseball.

Because Randy was five and in Kindergarten, he was eligible to try out for the tee-ball team at the local park. Everyone who wanted to play was accepted, but going through tryouts made it more real for the kids. After the first day he asked me if I thought he would make it and I answered that I wasn't sure. After day two of tryouts he announced to me that he knew he was going to make the team.

That confidence was short-lived, as Randy was not a confident boy. He had lived with an alcoholic mother and crack cocaine addicted father until he was four years old, and that had ended after the father flew into a rage one day and beat Randy and his mother almost to death. The social workers made me look at the photographs taken by the police at the scene and later at the hospital and the anger that moved up inside of me was like nothing I had ever experienced. After he was released from the hospital he went to live with an aunt and her teenage sons, one of whom molested Randy regularly until he finally told someone what was happening. So it was not surprising that he had trust issues with people, primarily with men.

I still maintained that baseball was a part of the solution for getting Randy back on track socially and emotionally, and our twice weekly practices and Saturday morning games were just the right thing for him. He desperately wanted to play and be on the team, so he allowed himself to trust me to make sure he would not be harmed. I assured him that I would be there every minute and that we would never be alone with anyone from the team or the local park where we met.

The world of children's team sports was new to me, as it had been quite different when my stepchildren were growing up. Now every child received a trophy at the end of the season and it was more about building self-esteem and confidence than about increasing skills and winning games. In Randy's case, this was the perfect scenario.

He was big for his age and the coaches quickly realized this did not mean he was a natural athlete. He was awkward and clumsy and it took many hours of practice before he could connect with the ball. This was tee-ball, so that meant the ball was placed atop a plastic stand and he was given three swings to hit it. It was more like thirty-three, but the other kids and the adults were patient with him.

One boy said to him one day "Why doesn't your dad practice with you?" and I quickly jumped up from my spot on the grass to make sure this didn't escalate into either a verbal or a physical altercation. But Randy looked at the boy and answered calmly, "My dad's in recovery from drugs and alcohol and my Ma is taking care of me for now. She'll be happy to practice with me." My sunglasses hid the tears welling up in my eyes and I nodded yes so that he could see I was in total agreement to this plan.

So practice we did, and Randy's life improved along with his game.

The most noticeable change in Randy was in his relationships with the coaches and the fathers whom we spent time with three times a week. In Randy's previous world men were not to be trusted. Both his father and grandfather were alcoholics and his father had also become addicted to crack cocaine before Randy could remember. This meant that either of these men could be nice at one moment and violent in the next. Randy had learned to watch for the signs and stay out of the way.

"When my Dad goes to the store for a six-pack, I pretend I don't feel good and ask Mom to put me to bed," he shared with me one day. We had driven by the liquor store in his old neighborhood and that jogged the memory.

I never knew quite what to say to him on these occasions, but just listening and acknowledging him seemed to suffice.

The baseball dads were so much different than what he had known at home. Everything was about their kids and the experiences they were having, and baseball was the perfect backdrop for the life lessons they wished to impart on these boys. It took them a week or so to understand Randy's situation and I allowed this to unfold in as natural a way as possible. Once they internalized what this little fellow had seen and experienced in his five short years on earth they became his biggest advocates.

One day at batting practice one of the coaches was helping Randy with his stance and holding the bat properly and I heard him say "That's right, son" to him. Randy froze, and looking up at this man he had only known for a few weeks he said in all seriousness "Are you another one of my Dads?" The coach paused, smiled, and went on to explain to him that in baseball, everyone is related. Randy liked that answer and began referring to his teammates as his "baseball brothers."

The season progressed and the tee-ball team had its share of wins and losses. Randy seemed almost oblivious to this state of affairs in the beginning, and one day announced to me that "winning is way more fun than losing" in baseball. I agreed and then praised him for being a good sport and focusing on improving his skills and being a good team player instead of only caring about the win.

Baseball strategies carried over into Randy's academic life as well. In his Kindergarten class his math skills improved significantly, and he told his teacher it was because you have to know math if you're going to play baseball. This activity also helped him to fit in better with his classmates, most of whom were involved in team sports and other activities away from school.

I volunteered to be "snack mom" as often as possible, freeing up the other mothers and siblings to be present for the team. It was awesome to watch as they included Randy in every detail of the proceedings so that he would be fully immersed in the world of baseball, albeit from the tee-ball point of view.

Over our fourteen weeks together Randy improved, to the point where he became a fair batter and a very good left fielder. He would swell with pride when they chanted "Randy, Randy, Randy!" after a good play.

I still have the team picture from Randy's tee-ball team that year. It's bittersweet, as he left my care just three days after receiving his end of season trophy at the final pizza party. But this interaction with people and a game that had been completely foreign to him at the start and the most special part of his life by the end left an indelible make upon his future. And to this day, when I drive by a local park and see little boys playing baseball I always send a silent "You can do it" to them through the fence and across the field.

Second Inning

Joel Warshawer

There is Crying in Baseball

I love baseball.

I grew up in the middle of a lifelong baseball game in the projects in the Sheepshead Bay section of Brooklyn, New York in the 1960s. There is a magic and a beauty in the game that is so different than all other sports.

There is no clock hovering over the game. There is a guarantee that your team gets to bat, without the fear that time is running out. There are nine innings in major league baseball, but only seven in the Little League.

I was nine years old when I was playing in the Little League, on a team that hadn't won a game in two years, while my twelve year old brother's team was a first place team that went to the city finals.

It was frustrating for me to be on a losing team. I was used to winning, because my favorite professional baseball team was the New York Yankees, who were always winning.

Our team had many games scheduled after school, usually at 5pm. It was on one of those days that my team was losing in the bottom of the last inning, but I was up at the plate with the bases loaded, with a chance to tie the game or go ahead. I was hoping to help our team to get our first win.

I felt the pressure, but though I wasn't a great hitter, I had an excellent on base percentage. I was very short, and got walked a lot because of my small strike zone. I felt glad to be up at bat with a chance to finally get a win. It was getting gray, as the sun kept sinking as the game wore on. I could see my father in the stands rooting me on.

The pitches kept coming, as it kept getting darker, the pressure was building, as I worked the count to 3 and 2. A full count, another ball and we would be tied, that was my first goal, to avoid another loss.

My hands were gripping the bat tighter with every pitch, as I felt that I was on the verge of saving my team from another loss. Bases loaded, just another ball I thought as the pitch came in low and hit home plate. "Wow, great I thought, ball four," except that the umpire called it strike three, calling me out, ending the game.

What? How can that be? It hit home plate, that's always called a ball.

Everyone started walking off the field, except me. For the first time in my life I questioned an adult.

I asked him, "How can that be a strike? It hit home plate." He ignored me, as I kept asking him, and soon I started crying. I then felt a hand on my shoulder, as I continued crying.

I turned around to see who was trying to console me. It was my father, I cried to him, "How could that be a strike?"

He hugged me for one of the few times in my life and said, "It's over. Let's go to Jahn's Ice Cream Parlor to drown our sorrows."

We went there to drown our sorrows in our ice cream sodas.

It's been over fifty years since that day, but I can still feel the heartbreak of making the final out, and losing that game. I can also remember how much healing that ice cream soda gave me.

But Dad, This is the World Series

Joel Warshawer

There has always been baseball in my life. Long before VCRs and DVRs and ESPN, there was baseball. But on one sunny afternoon in October of 1964 I was being denied my right watch my favorite team, the New York Yankees play a World Series game.

On this perfect autumn day with my New York Yankees playing against the St. Louis Cardinals, I was so excited to watch the game.

It was an afternoon game. My father had invited my Uncle Lennie over to watch the game with him. The problem for me was that it was a school day for me. In those days, all of the World Series games were played in the daytime. I just assumed that my father would allow me to take off half the day of school so that I could watch the game. He knew how much I loved baseball and this was my favorite team playing in the World Series.

My father wasn't usually in charge of making decisions about letting us stay home from school because he was working. But his company had been on strike, and my mother was now working, leaving him in charge of the kids. I would walk nine blocks home from school to eat lunch there.

So on this day, coming home for lunch I saw my father preparing snacks for the game. He was cooking hot dogs, making French fries, putting chips and pretzels in bowls. There were also bowls of chocolates, and pistachio nuts. There was ice cream in the freezer, and plenty of bottles of Coke.

He gave me one of the hot dogs for lunch, and said that I should start getting ready to get back to school. I said "What about the game, can I stay home to watch it?"

He quickly said no. As a kid, I never asked for, or demanded anything from either of my parents, but I asked once again "Can I please watch the game?"

He again quickly said no, but now was getting angry with me. I was angry myself, surveying the snacks spread out all around the living room. A buffet of junk food, perfect for watching a baseball game.

He raised his voice this time and yelled at me, "Go back to school, now!"

I said, "But please Dad, this is the World Series."

I was now desperate as the game was about to start, without me getting to watch it. I was thinking of taking a desperate measure, and took the only one that came to my mind. I went into the bathroom, took a red Bic pen out of my pocket, and drew red dots all over my face and up and down both of my arms, to make it appear that I had the Measles.

When I came out of the bathroom, I told my father that I was feeling sick, and that I thought I might have the Measles. He quickly examined me and his face turned a bright read with anger. He began yelling at me to get back to school now, and to stop faking it. He then grabbed my arms one at a time and wiped off the ink spots. I started crying.

He looked at me crying and hesitated, and then quietly said, "Go to the bathroom and wash off the ink, and you can stay home and watch the game."

I won that day, even though my team lost.

Third Inning

Phil London and Georgia Cordill-London

Boston's Casey at the Bat

Our 12-year old, Jake, had a pretty bad year. He'd been suffering from a chronic illness. Not easy for a sports nut kid. He sat out his Little League season in the spring and missed a lot of school. As fall approached, he improved. What better way to celebrate a Boston-born boy feeling good than a late September Sox game at Fenway.

September 23, 2003 to be precise. A perfect evening during the best time of year in New England. And Jake's beloved Red Sox were in a pennant race with, of course, the Yankees. Every game mattered now.

We picked this game, against the Baltimore Orioles, because, while Jake from Boston was a Red Sox fan, Mom grew up in Maryland and went to high school in Aberdeen with Orioles star Cal Ripken. Dad, a 3rd-generation Yankee fan, was suffering through deciding whom to root against.

None of us remember much about the first 8 innings. Into the top of the 9th, the visiting Orioles were up 3-2. Our memories fuse collectively at a moment in that inning as the Orioles batted. With two men on base, an easily fielded single was hit at right fielder Gabe Kapler. The stadium collectively relaxed because it was clear the runners would be held and no runs would score. That was, until Kapler made a boneheaded play, letting an easy ball scoot by him. By the time the Red Sox came up in the bottom of the 9th, they found themselves down 5-2.

The Sox were strong enough that season to make a 3-2 game interesting, but now they trailed by 3. If not for the events that transpired over the next 45 minutes, the three of us today, 15 years later, would not remember every pitch, every act soon to occur.

As the Red Sox batted in the bottom of the ninth, Boston manager Terry Francona made his moves. Pinch hitter. Pinch hitter. A hit. A walk. A stolen base. The Sox had Nomar on second and Varitek on third. Now, with two outs, bottom of the ninth, second baseman Todd Walker made his way to the plate.

Even the most determined Red Sox fans remember little about Walker, who played only that one 2003 season in Boston. We remember him though. A ball. A strike. Ball. Ball. A weak foul. The count is 3-2, with two outs in the 9th. We probably don't have to explain what happened next, but even Yankee fan Dad finds himself standing and cheering, and we're going to extra innings.

You might think Walker's 9th inning heroics are worthy of this story, but this story is not about Walker. For leading off in the bottom of the 10th, in a 5-5 game, in the midst of a pennant chase was David Ortiz.

Big Papi was in his prime in 2003. The expression "strode" is often used casually in baseball, but in this moment, Big Papi STRODE to the plate. Dad elbowed Jake in the ribs. "Watch this! He is locked in!"

He took the first pitch. Called Strike. Then a couple of balls. Papi stepped out of the batter's box. Spit in one hand then slapped them both together. Disgusting, but his signature move. Then he stepped back into the box and he literally looked nine feet tall.

Some athletes just are larger than life. Their ability to own the moment is otherworldly. Some really are worthy of the adulation of a 12 year-old battling an illness.

They say baseball brings generations together. As the ball rose against that crisp, beautiful New England sky, disappearing over Fenway's Green Monster, a moment we shared will be shared by us forever. Amazing that it works that way.

Epilogue

2003 would end ignominiously for the Red Sox, losing to the Yankees in extra innings in Game 7 of the American League Championship on an unlikely home run by Aaron Boone. But their great 2003 season portended what was to come as the Red Sox, fielding almost that same roster, would in 2004 finally shatter the 86 year old Curse of the Bambino.

Many of these same players are still in the news. Boone is the manager of the Yankees. Kapler, who booted that single in right, is the manager of the Philadelphia Phillies.

And Big Papi has retired after many more great seasons and after creating many more moments for families to cherish forever. Ours was that evening, September 23, 2003.

Fourth Inning

Rex Bohachewski

Keep Going!

I was in Grade 9 and we were playing a game of baseball during P.E. (Physical Education) one day. Due to my size (tiny compared to the rest of the kids) and my eyesight (not the greatest), P.E. was not my best subject- I was definitely not a star athlete. The effort was there on my part (thankfully) so I enjoyed the class.

As I nervously waited for my turn at bat (I did not want to strike out swinging), I was watching the pitches as best as I could (so really not seeing anything, but I felt better thinking I knew where they were going). I thought I would know where the ball would be as I swung wildly and blindly (literally) at my time at bat.

When I finally got up to bat, the pitch that I received was a much slower pitch than I expected. (Thank you to my P.E. teacher who was the umpire behind me who indicated to the pitcher to give me an easier pitch to swing at as I could not see anything coming at me. To this day I believe I got the easier pitch at his direction.)

I swung and missed the first pitch. The second pitch I connected. With no idea where the ball went, I ran to first base and stopped. My teammates were yelling at me to keep going. So I did, still not knowing where the ball was. I got to second base and stopped. Again my teammates were yelling at me to keep going, so I did, running to third base where I stopped. At this point my teammates where still yelling at me to keep going, and I still didn't know where the ball was. So I ran home. As I crossed home plate, the ball hit the back of my leg as I lifted my leg off of the plate. My teammates were cheering as they crowded around me. I had just "hit" a home run.

Later, if I remember correctly, I found out that the fielders had difficulty with the ball and that my fellow classmates on the other team had difficultly catching the ball at each of the bases, so the ball was being "thrown away" at the bases that I was arriving at meaning the other team was constantly chasing down the ball at each base while I kept advancing through 1st, 2nd, 3rd, and finally home.

I know I had some "help" with that "home run", but it makes for a great moment (and story) for a tiny skinny kid who wears glasses and who was not very good at sports, one I will never forget. It meant a lot to a kid in Grade 9.

Fifth Inning

Donna Kozik

Big League Ball & Me

My first baseball game was a double-header in Pittsburgh when the Steelers and the Pirates still shared a stadium. My dad "drove bus" for the Corry Area School District and one Saturday morning found a group of high school students, my mom, my eight-year-old sister and my ten-year-old self bouncing around in a big yellow school bus and down I-79 to Three Rivers Stadium.

My more vivid memories from that day include getting a canary yellow and black striped sun visor with the eye-patched mascot on the front (more practical than a foam finger) to wear with pride. Those were the days when parents and kids weren't attached at the hip and at the start of the fourth inning of the first game Teresa and I were left to our own devices in the stadium seats while Mom and Dad went for a walk-around.

During the game, and led by the stadium organist, a chant started. But what were they saying? Teresa and I couldn't figure it out exactly, but it sounded like "Let's go NUTS!" So we shouted it along with the rest of the fans--with gusto. (Only later did we find the proper phrase was "Let's go BUCS!")

Since that day, baseball peeked in and out of my life. Dad always watched the playoffs and World Series, making sure we were all sitting in front of the Curtis Mathes stereo TV when the national anthem played. Right after college a friend who worked at a bank got tickets to their company suite and I enjoyed another game with a better view and adult beverages.

Then my writing work led to a job as a newspaper for my hometown weekly, The Union City-Waterford Times Leader. After that was a corporate communications job at Erie Insurance where the activities club organized trips (coach buses this time!) to see the Cleveland Indians play in their brand new Jacobs Field. We were up so high I felt if I looked down at just the right angle I could tip right onto the field. A couple of friends and I got mitts and would go out and "toss around the pill" at lunch, too.

But it wasn't until I moved to San Diego that I really became a true baseball fan. I decided to start my own business as a book-writing coach, which meant loads of long hours in front of the computer, usually well into the evening. The TV kept me company, but it's not like you can write and follow an episode of "Law & Order." At the time I was talking to a guy who was always talking baseball (he was wearing a San Francisco Giants cap long before it was cool) and decided to tune in myself. "Donna, you have to root for the home team," he said, so I became a San Diego Padres fan. I have to say, it wasn't the exciting plays that kept me watching, but rather the broadcast team of Mark "Mud" Grant and Matt Vasgersian. They were my company as I wrote web copy and planned teleseminars to share with my audience.

I found baseball to be the perfect writing background as the crack of the bat alerts you to look up and see what's going on. Mark and Matt's corny jokes and banter entertained me (I'm easily amused) through some long seasons and now I find myself having been a Padres fan for more than 15 years.

Friends and Baseball

My love of baseball has rubbed off—or been forced upon—others in my life, too.

There was the April 17, 2008 game my friend Marji and I went to. The Rockies and Padres were tied at the end of 9 innings. We stayed for the 10th, but no one scored so we left Petco Park. As soon as we got in the car Marji said "turn on the game!" We listened to Ted Leitner call the 11th and 12th innings. No more scoring. At my house we turned on the tube and watched the 13th, 14th and 15th innings.

Marji had to work the next day so she headed home after verifying the radio station where she could hear the end of the game in her car. She lives an hour away, so when she got home we chatted over instant messaging during the 19th, 20th, and 21st innings. The Rockies finally scored a run at the top of 22nd (I believe our shortstop was pitching at the time) and the Padres couldn't answer in the bottom half so the game finally ended. My favorite part of the whole thing was the three "seventh inning stretches" we had – one in the 7th and then the 14th and then the 21st. It tired the squad out for weeks to come, though, adding more numbers to the loss column.

For years I've wondered what I would do when a foul ball came my way. They zing at you a lot faster than you might think. I was at a game in August 2016 with my sister and brother-in-law on the first base side when one came sailing down from up above. Turns out, Teresa ducked and I stood tall and reached. I'm still surprised I didn't get it—that honor went to the man in front of me. I'll be ready next time! (Might even take my glove.)

I have a friend who told me he got two free tickets to a Chicago Cubs game at Wrigley field. He and his wife went, looked around, stayed two innings and left. My mouth was agape. First, it's Wrigley! Second, it's Wrigley! Third, no matter the match up, you never know when a no-hitter is going to happen. (That's why you never refuse tickets to a game.) I tried to explain to him the intricacies of baseball and why you go and stay, but my second minute brought back memories of the second inning for him and he stopped listening. That's OK—more for the rest of us!

There's another friend who has loved baseball longer than I have. Her grandfather was an usher and back in the early days had team members and coaches over for dinner. It's always fun to go to a game with her as she shares stories passed down from the generations before. She was in high school the last time the Padres were at the World Series (before you look it up, we've never taken the top honor) and had her favorite players that now pepper the "history videos" shown between innings. We've sat everywhere around the ballpark where there's always a good view. She says I talk "just enough" to not distract from the game, yet keep our catch-up conversation going.

Why do I love baseball? Well, I'm a news junky, so these days it's a nice escape. To turn on the game where optimism reigns supreme and "God Bless America" is played on Sunday afternoons soothes my soul. It's also a form of meditation to pull me into another world after a busy work day on the phone and teaching people how to write and publish books. I've been known to "zone out" and just let it envelope me in its history and soft easy play. There's always something interesting happening, even if it's subtle, like the announcement of a pitcher throwing their 10,000th pitch (I saw Jake Peavey do that) or a rookie getting his first hit (Anthony Rizzo) and the guys joking as they pretend to throw the coveted ball back into the stands. Most of all, through household moves and relationships that come and go, baseball remains a constant. A time to relax and take in a game at a big league ballpark—even on what is now a flat screen TV—still brings a zing of anticipation and fun to me.

Donna Kozik is an award-winning author who shows others how to write a book "fast and easy" and use it as a "big business card." She does this with her Write a Book in a Weekend program. She also gets authors started in speaking with her Speaking to Authority program. Get your free book planner at http://FreeBookPlanner.com.

Sixth Inning

Jack Marriott

A Play So Rare It May Never Have Happened Before!

Die-hard Baseball Fans love statistics. I love statistics! Here are some of my favourites.

In 1927 Babe Ruth hit 60 home runs in a single season. That record held until 1961 when Roger Maris hit 61 home runs, although purists would say that the '61 season was longer and therefore Babe's record still stood. Babe Ruth actually ended his career in 1935 with the record of 714 home runs. Eventually this was shattered by Hank Aaron, a contemporary of Roger Maris, who hit 755 lifetime home runs before he retired in 1976. And finally, Barry Bonds career ended in 2007 when he hit his last home run which was number 762 in a controversial career.

This story is about a statistic that is so rare, yet so profound, that it may never have been recorded in major league baseball. Although a future major league baseball player had pitched in the game it occurred in.

Baseball has been my life-long passion. Growing up in Canada, I lived with my sister, Mom and Dad in an apartment suite across the street from Lord Roberts elementary school in Vancouver's West End. As early as age 6, I would start each day walking across the road, carrying my chipped old baseball bat, whatever ball I could find and my tattered baseball mitt with threadbare webbing and start hitting balls into the school fence.

The school yard was gravel, rocks and dirt with the odd weed attempting to claim its space in this barren ground. Eventually somebody else would show up and we would play catch for a bit and them played Five Hundred - a game where one person batted the ball and the other fielded the ball, if you caught the ball in the air you earned 100 points, on one bounce 75 points, on two bounces 50 points and 25 points for a ground ball and if you dropped a ball you got negative points on the same scale. When you earn 500 points you get to bat the ball. When there was four or more of us then we started playing "scrub" the slang term for any unorganized baseball game. I loved the crazy bounces on this rocky field, it made catching the ball challenging and fun. I wore my bruises and cuts proudly. I did this nearly every day for years rain or shine. I became a really good fielder, could catch anything and I credit that with my many years playing ball on this schoolyard.

On Saturday afternoons in the 1950's an American TV station had the Major League Baseball game of the week which I never missed. I'm talking black and white television. I also loved listening to and watching former baseball Hall of Fame pitcher Dizzy Dean as the colorful commentator, singing country medleys of songs from his youth in the Ozarks, and never allowing a vendor to walk by his broadcasting station without buying a hot dog and letting us viewers know how great it tasted.

Whilst watching these games on TV I found my lifelong hero. A young short stop was doing things no other short stop had ever done before - hitting lots of home runs! He was a young guy named Ernie Banks playing for the Chicago Cubs who spent most of their time in the basement of the National League, battling with Philadelphia to move out of last place every year in the mid to late 1950s. Despite playing on a last place team, Ernie was such an amazing baseball player in 1958 that he was voted the league's Most Valuable Player and was the first player to repeat the award in consecutive years in

1959. I've been a die-hard Chicago Cubs fan ever since. In fact, I was a Cubs fan long before it was fashionable to be a fan of the team who were dubbed the "Lovable Losers". The losing streak was finally over in 2016, nearly sixty years later when the Cubbies were victorious in the World Series, finally beating the "curse" that had lasted 108 years, in a nail-biting up and down series victory over the Cleveland Indians!!! What a game! What a day! A day I had waited my whole life to celebrate!

Inspired by Ernie Banks, I played the position of short stop for much of my baseball career. In High school when I was 15, I was asked to coach the girls Basketball team and then the girls Softball team (no slow pitch in those days)! Then the father of one of these girls phoned me and told me he had applied for and just received a franchise for Little League Baseball in the West End and asked me to coach one of these teams. Over the next 50 years I've coached all levels of baseball, softball and slow pitch. Including championships in league play, divisional play, provincials, and nationals.

There isn't much I haven't seen or experienced on a baseball field. Until this happened!

The year was 1994. The North Shore Twins, the team I was helping to coach was in the sweltering dry summer heat of the desert, during a premier baseball tournament in Kamloops, British Columbia, Canada. The boys were aged 16 to 18. We had a lot of games to play during this weekend tournament so we had to be strategic and limit the use of our pitchers in each game.

In this game we went with our star pitcher, Ryan Dempster. If you are a baseball fan you will recognize that name. Ryan went on to become an ace pitcher for the Miami Marlins, Chicago Cubs and Boston Red Sox. Ryan was a major league All Star and a World Series champion with the Boston Red Sox in his 17-year major league career. In fact, Ryan Dempster is considered the second best Canadian born major league Baseball pitcher behind another Cubbie, Hall of Famer Ferguson Jenkins.

Despite the heat, Ryan was in great form managing to throw six innings of shut-out baseball and we had a two to nothing lead going into the bottom half of the final inning of a seven inning game, the maximum number of innings for this tournament. The decision was made to sit Ryan at this point to preserve him for another game in this tournament. So now we had a dilemma - who were we going we going to put in to pitch the last inning in the hopes of closing out for the win. The decision was to put the second baseman in even though he hadn't pitched this year and that's when the game became interesting.

In no time at all, the bases were loaded with runners at first, second and third with nobody out. After whipping through six innings, now all of a sudden our team was potentially in big trouble. The tying run was at second base and the winning run at first. So the decision was to pull the pitcher and replace him with a new kid on the team whose name was Micah. And so Micah came in to pitch.

What a challenging position to be in! Just to recap: it's the last inning, we were leading 2 to 0, our new pitcher came in to the game with the bases loaded, nobody out and the possible tying run was at second base and the potential winning run was at first base.

Micah finishes his warm ups and the umpire yells out "Play Ball!" All the infielders started moving in with the strategy of preventing a run, by picking up a ground ball and throwing it to home for the force-out of the runner at third base. Micah picks up the sign from the catcher - a fast ball is called for. Micah nods goes into his wind up and throws a fastball over the center of the plate. The batter, takes a big swing and hits a hard ground ball right at the short stop.

Everybody on and off the diamond knew what was going to happen next. Sure enough, the short stop fields the ball cleanly and makes a hard throw to the catcher at home plate. The catcher caught the throw from the short stop, put his foot on home plate and the umpire called the runner from third base out at home plate!

Then the catcher quickly turned towards first base and fired the ball to the first baseman just getting the ball there in time to beat the batter by a foot step and the first base umpire called the batter

"Out!"

While all this excitement was going on, the runner from second base had his own game plan. As soon as that ball was hit, he sprinted as fast as he could towards third base and without looking back, stopping or slowing down his foot contacted third base and he continued at a full gallop like a thoroughbred horse at the Kentucky Derby destined to score a run at home plate. As he was now speeding towards home the first baseman caught a blurry glimpse out of the corner of his eye of the speeding opponent racing towards home.

The first baseman's baseball instincts took over and without wasting any time he immediately stepped towards home plate and reached back with all his strength to muster the hardest throw he could to return the ball to the catcher to stop the galloping base runner from scoring.

The pounding of the base runner's footsteps resounded in the ears of the catcher who was anxiously awaiting the return throw from the first baseman. Both the ball being thrown from first and the runner from second were on a collision course at home plate. The question now was which one would get there first.

The throw was hard but a little bit off and behind the catcher. So the catcher reached back, caught the ball and reacted in the only way he could. He caught the ball and dove arms stretched out towards the plate in an effort to tag the runner before the runner touched the plate.

As the catcher dove, the runner was barreling in at full bore without any the intention of sliding or attempting to avoid the tag. Now he looked like a Mack truck bearing down in full force on the catcher. He didn't even slide, rather like a football middle linebacker about to hit the quarterback, he barreled into the catcher just in front of the home plate. The collision was so intense that he knocked the catcher back six feet in the air and he landed on his butt with a resounding thud followed by a rising dust cloud caused by the impact. We were all temporarily blinded by the dust, out of which a glove with a ball in it appeared as the catcher maintaining his composure sitting on his rump, was holding it up for the umpire to see. And the umpire saw the ball in the catcher's glove and declared with a roar "Out!!!"

Whew!

That was a triple play to end the game.

But here's the thing. Once in a long while you'll see triple plays, usually something like runners at first and second or bases loaded and the ball is hit to the third baseman, who touches third ahead of the runner and throws to second baseman who touches second base ahead of the runner who throws to first base who touches first base ahead of the batter. And there you have a triple play.

This was a very different triple play. It went from short stop to home forcing the runner from third base out at home, then the catcher threw the ball to first base where the batter was out before reaching first base and then the first baseman threw the ball home to the catcher who was able to tag the runner from second base before he touched home plate for the third out of the play. A very rare triple play indeed. But that's not it. Well not entirely. If you didn't get it, I totally understand. Only the odd person on the baseball field and only the really baseball-wise people in the stands got it!

As we were celebrating the victory on the field and walking off in the merriment of winning the game. I put my arm around Micah's shoulders and asked him if he understood the significance of what had just happened. He looked at me and said "Yah, we won the game." Oh, you got to love that laid back attitude of the young pitcher. I said to him "Yes we did and that was very important. But there was something even more significant."

Micah said "Yah, I know, we won the game on a triple play!"

I responded "And..."

He shook his head and said "What?"

I said "Micah, in my 40 years of playing, coaching and watching baseball games I've seen quite a few triple plays. But, this was the rarest thing I've ever seen in a baseball game."

I continued "What you did was so rare it may never have happened before. You came into the game in the last inning. The bases were loaded and nobody out. You threw one pitch, preserved the victory and got the close. I've never seen a game where the closer comes in with nobody out, throws one pitch and ends the game with 3 outs.

Micah said "Wow! I didn't realize that!

And that my friends, is my story is about a statistic that is so rare, and so profound, that I don't believe it has ever been recorded in major league baseball.

Jack Marriott is a Chicago Cubs fan, a lifelong baseball player, and a coach.

Seventh Inning

Cheryl A. Major

Closing the Sale at Fenway Park

In the summer of 1994 I sold Dan Duquette a home in Acton, Massachusetts. Dan was the General Manager of the Red Sox at the time, and I enjoyed working with him. Although he received mixed reviews during his time there (Boston sports fans are notoriously mercurial, fickle and just plain tough), I found him to be direct and of his word; I liked him very much and enjoyed the time I spent with him. He was a no nonsense person who did not suffer fools, a quality for which I have great respect! I always knew where I stood with Dan, and I knew he appreciated my efforts to take care of him and help him make a great home choice.

It was also funny because I'm very good at keeping my mouth shut about my clients' identities, a good quality if you're working with high profile clients who don't want their home searches and information share widely. The listing broker was a huge baseball fan and had no idea who was coming with me to see the house. When Dan and I showed up, it was comical! The broker fell all over himself and couldn't believe who the potential buyer was. He even chided me for not telling him the buyer was Dan Duquette!

The transaction went very smoothly, we were on track to close, and then I got the news...Dan had invited us to close the transaction at Fenway Park!

We all have events that stand out in our memories, and for me, this is one of them. I remember the day was rainy, the traffic driving in to Boston was slow and so the closing was a little later than expected. I had been given directions to drive in to the garage area under the park where the ball players and the administrators parked. I got out of my car and looked around me in amazement. The ceiling was very tall, and in my memory it was a cavernous place; dark and almost like a basement, but that may be magnified by the years in between. When you drove in you had to navigate the supports – these big concrete pillars, and I was directed where to park.

Because it was during the afternoon and not at game time, the park was pretty deserted. It was so odd, having been there before for ball games, to see it so empty.

The walk to the closing room was down halls and corridors few of us mere mortals had walked, and I was acutely aware of the privilege I was enjoying. I thought of the ball players like Babe Ruth, Ted Williams, Carl Yastrzemski and Jim Rice who had walked in this same place years ago.

Finally I arrived at the conference room on the top floor, and what I remember most is that room in which the closing was held. It was a large room with walls on three sides; the fourth wall was all glass and overlooked the ball field. There was a long conference table, and we were seated around it. When I sat down and looked up, the view of Fenway Park was amazing! I looked to the left and panned across the view of the field. It was huge and so very green. You cannot imagine the charm and beauty of Fenway Park if you haven't experienced it from this height, from this perspective. The rain had stopped and was now a light drizzle. I think the dampness made the grass look even greener. There were ball players taking practice and people milling around on the field.

Dan had a ball player who was waiting to meet with him on the field, so he signed his paperwork and excused himself to go meet with the player. I wish I could remember who it was and if the player ended up with the Red Sox, but I can't. I can tell you it was a special memory to see Dan walk out onto the field and meet with the coaches and the player being interviewed.

My trip that time to Fenway Park was one few people would ever have. I was so fortunate to get an inside visit to the iconic Fenway Park!

Cheryl A Major, CNWC

Cheryl A Major lives in Westford, Massachusetts and is a Certified Nutrition and Wellness Consultant. Her TV show, Thin Strong Healthy, airs on WestfordCat and is an offshoot of her blog http://ThinStrongHealthy.com. Cheryl is also a full time residential Realtor with Coldwell Banker with more than twenty-five years experience.

Seventh Inning Stretch

Connie Ragen Green

Silent Baseball

You don't hear a sound when you watch silent baseball.

Not the commentators' shared thoughts, their opinions, any predictions, or even some valuable references.

Not the crack of the bat when it connects with the ball.

Not the roar of the crowd when almost anything occurs.

Unvoiced, no wood crashing against leather, no laughter, no cheers, no whistles.

And you miss the visuals as well.

The players communicating with looks, glances, and stares.

The catcher "talking" to the pitcher with finger signals.

The excellent plays and the awkward near misses.

The batter taking his time to get his body in just the right position and his mind in exactly the right place to accept the next pitch.

The "wave", the crowd singing along during the 7th inning stretch, the hats, clothes, and the makeup of the fans in the stands.

The spitting! The fights! The rain!

Silent baseball doesn't tell the whole story - that's for sure.

But the numbers do not lie - not ever.

Just the facts, and nothing but the facts.

I imagine the commentator sharing a personal story from 1998.

I picture the catcher's signals as his fingers fly beneath his glove.

I visualize the batter running confidently to first...and carefully on to second base, and then stealing third!

I silently cheer when the opposing team's pitcher balks.

But in silent baseball I have to wait to read the details.

...a 88.4 mph curve ball

...runner out at third base

...a 94.7 mph knuckle curve

...runner on first base

...86.8 mph four seam fast ball

...runners on first and second

...mound advisory

...a 101.4 mph four seam fast ball

Baseball is a noisy game, but silent baseball on my tablet works when given no other choice.

Just the facts, and nothing but the facts.

Dreaming of Yankee Stadium

Connie Ragen Green

I dreamt I was on the D train headed to Yankee Stadium.

Standing up, gripping tightly to the pole in the middle of the car,

Surrounded by people who may be going to the same place.

The conductor calls out that we are approaching the 161st Street Station, Yankee Stadium, and the train screeches to a halt.

The cars all empty, as everyone was going to the game that day.

Then I am in the stands, sitting in the seat next to some friends.

It's my birthday and this was their gift to me. I say a silent "thank you."

It's the fifth inning with the score one to one, and Didi Gregorius homers off a pitch from Seattle Mariners' Marco Gonzales. As he rounds second base it begins to rain and my friend pulls out a plastic bag to cover our heads.

Sir Didi reaches home plate, the score is now two to one, the crowd goes wild, the rain comes down harder, and now we are at an Italian restaurant two blocks from the stadium, celebrating my birthday and the Yankees' win.

Eighth Inning

Clay Morgan

The Diamond-Shaped Classroom at Fairview Park

I pitched the greatest game of my entire life one summer night when I was eleven years old.

Everything worked for me that evening. I couldn't miss the strike zone. When I did miss with my pitch, so did the batter. When they roped line drives straight back at me I snagged them out of the air with ease. I struck out the biggest kid on the other team three straight times.

Then I went home and cried.

Now, I wasn't a super melodramatic kid. The only other time I had cried happened on the field one time when I was a little right fielder, and my grandparents came to watch me play at Fairview Park. It wasn't the only time they came, but that night felt special. With the game on the line in the final inning, the ball came my way as the potential winning run rounded third base to touch home plate and send us to a loss.

I stepped toward the catcher and whipped my skinny left arm like a fly swatter. Eyeballs all over the place popped like corks. The ball beat the runner. My catcher held on. The game was saved. We went into extra innings. I felt like a hero.

Until...

An inning or two later, a routine fly ball came my way. It came to me, the kid with the amazing arm who had saved the game like Roberto Clemente would have. The little white orb seemed to soar through the night forever. I had time to think, and that was not good. By the time the lazy fly ball reached me its red stitches looked like the angry eyebrows of a dragon.

I dropped the ball.

We lost.

I felt like a goat.

I wasn't the only one who cried and tried to mask the tears from my grandparents even as they smeared into the dirt on my face. I remember my grandma smiling and my grandfather offering some reassuring words but knew I had failed them and everybody else.

We teammates couldn't look each other in the eyes. We felt the shame of failure. Still, such moments are routine during childhood. Such hard losses are to be expected.

But this other night at Fairview Park, the one I want to tell you about, became anything but routine. On that warm, summer night the concept of loss took on a new, terrifying meaning. That's the night I pitched my greatest game ever but was never the same again afterward.

~*~*~

I grew up in a small town, the kind of community where generations of folks who attended high school together reconvened on sun-soaked bleachers every Saturday morning and on some weeknights. In our town, they perched on rusting metal rows to watch their kids and grandchildren play on fields they helped build.

Aside from the occasional crazy dad—typically about one per team—most spectators enjoyed the camaraderie around games. With good nature, they cheered on their team while also supporting good sportsmanship from the opposition.

You would get to know some of the kids and their parents in this way. Some of the children were punks, usually because some of the parents were jerks. Other than that, everyone cheered for everyone.

There was one player in the league that everyone seemed to know. His name was Shawn. He was the biggest player in the league, an unfortunate side effect of the deadly disease threatening to shorten his young life.

The illness was aplastic anemia, a rare disease in which stem cells inside the bone marrow are damaged and unable to regenerate. Marie Curie and Eleanor Roosevelt died because of aplastic anemia.

What I most remember about Shawn was how small the bat looked in his hand, and how tight the helmet fit around the thick hair atop his head. He may have played first base for his team that night, but memories are slippery, untrustworthy things, so that recollection might be fiction.

I was left-handed, a southpaw as they say in baseball. I don't remember how many kids I struck out that night or if I gave up any runs. I don't even recall how many hits I had on offense. I only remember the paradox of the overall result—we won, and I was devastated.

By the time Shawn stepped into the batter's box, I knew who he was. My first time through the lineup did not feature a sympathetic approach. I wanted to do well. I wanted mom, aunt, and coach to be proud. I especially wanted the jerk dad from our team to not have anything to run his mouth about because the only thing I hated more than when he yelled at his son was when he criticized me.

So, when Shawn struck out that first time, it was routine. He wasn't the only hitter I fanned. But I remember his awkward stance. The disease that replaced blood stem cells with fat robbed its victim of coordination. Shawn's swing was labored and not timed well. He took his swings, but they weren't close to making contact.

The second time I faced him, I took something off my pitches. Once more, he swung and missed three quick times, and that was that. He didn't react in anger, and his team and fans offered supportive cheers every time he tried. But I was not okay with how bad he looked up there. With how bad I had made him look.

I considered walking him by throwing four straight pitches way outside the strike zone, but even at my young age there seemed to be something cruel in that kind of condescending pity. He was there to compete, to escape from a deadly battle already defining his life. Who was I to snatch that chance away?

His third trip to the plate looked similar to the first two but with one exception. By that point, I was lobbing soft throws in there like it was batting practice. I always had a good arm, accurate from the outfield. I decided that if he couldn't hit what I threw, then I would just aim for his bat.

I never worked so hard to throw a ball where a person's bat would be less than two seconds later.

He swung and missed at the first pitch. He always went down swinging. As I adjusted my cap and traced lines in the dirt with the tip of my shoe, I muttered a silent prayer. "Please God, just let him hit this one."

I gripped the ball in my glove and came set, secretly plotting all the ways I could make sure he made it safely to first base if he happened to hit a weak dribbler in my direction. Perhaps I would field the ball and throw it nine feet over the first basemen's reach. By that point, I wasn't even looking at my catcher or his glove. I focused only on where Shawn's bat would soon be. I finally had an idea of how he timed his swing and instinctively considered the timing of it all. Then I threw the pitch.

Shawn swung. The head of his bat came through about chest high, exactly where my pitch was heading. He made contact. A loud PING resounded throughout the park, and the ball launched off his bat like a rocket. He was bigger and more powerful than anyone I had faced, so the trajectory surprised me.

His swing was a fraction of a second late, so the ball sailed towards the opposite field, right field. Our collective eyes shot towards the sky over first base. Excited cheers popped up from all around. Shawn dropped his bat and began running, his steps uneven yet eager.

"Foul ball!" yelled the umpire.

The ball had been driven far but foul, outside the white line of fair play. But nothing about the situation seemed fair to me.

Less than a minute later, I had thrown one more strike, which Shawn missed. Another strikeout. The catcher tossed the ball back to me as Shawn returned to his team's dugout. He didn't even look sad. I was crestfallen.

On a regulation ballfield, a pitching mound sits sixty feet and six inches away from home plate. In youth baseball, they often shorten that distance a few inches, but you've still got more than the length of a school bus between you and the hitters. Once the game ends, however, the teams line up to shake hands and learn something about sportsmanship.

Normally, it would have been satisfying to go through that line after pitching such a great victory. I should have been reveling in the respect seen in the eyes of the kids I had gotten the better of that game. I should've enjoyed the way opposing coaches gave me props for tossing a "heckuva game." But on that night at Fairview Park, I dreaded the handshake line more than ever.

No longer fifty feet apart, I looked past the kids as we performed our perfunctory high fives and chanted "good game good game good game..." Shawn approached from the other direction. Twenty feet away. Then ten feet. Five, four, three...

I braced, wrestling with a compulsion to apologize to him. But saying sorry felt akin to intentionally walking him.

Two, one...

As we connected in that slow procession, I finally saw him up close. It seemed impossible that he was only 12-years-old. A dark thought flickered through my mind about how he was unlikely to live long enough to graduate high school. I don't think I said anything as our hands touched.

We arrived home just past twilight. I maintained silence for fear of what might happen if I tried to speak. I felt like a dam was about to burst inside me. I couldn't stay in the house, not with all those bright lights on.

In the backyard, all I could think of was Shawn, and how he was going to die, and how I didn't do anything to help him succeed. How I had made him fail.

"Why did tonight have to be the best game I ever pitched?" I pleaded in anger to the dark sky as I paced the yard and drifted to the abandoned lot across the street.

Who knows how long I sat on the stoop of the old company store, tears etching grooves in the dirt on my face.

My oldest sister Bethany came out and consoled me. I don't remember what she said, but I needed to tell someone why I was so upset, and she listened. Then she comforted me with some big sister words. Seeing how I was wrestling with majorly adult thoughts for one of the first times, she countered with some adult words of her own. Eventually I smiled, and then we were laughing.

I like to imagine that as we went back to the house that night, she was dragging me along in a hug like Brand did for Mikey in The Goonies after their front porch heart to heart. It didn't happen like that probably, but that's what I like to imagine.

I decided to quit playing baseball--the great passion of my childhood--around age twelve. Shawn couldn't play ball too much longer either. But he kept fighting his greater battle until it took his life at the age of fifteen.

He was laid to rest under a large, lovely stone on the backside of the cemetery where I worked for four years between high school and college. I visited with him many times back there on the sun-drenched bank of Section 13.

Sometimes I talked about baseball, but instead of apologizing for striking him out, I told him he didn't deserve to be dealt such a terrible hand in life. Every glance at his plot became a reminder to always take my swings and live well.

~*~*~

I used to think baseball fields should be shaped like tears instead of diamonds.

With all due respect to Tom Hanks and the legendary film A League of Their Own, there is most definitely crying in baseball. I know because that sport was the first love of my life, and first loves can always break your heart.

But there was a lot of learning in those tears. So many of the early lessons learned in life were, for me, generated in classrooms shaped like ballfields.

Baseball is life. Because of the game, I first learned about teamwork and adversity and perseverance. After taking a fastball off my right knee one year, I had to learn courage. When I struck out four times myself one night, the line was drawn in the dirt. I would either become mentally stronger, maintain composure, and get back in there, or I would have to quit.

I came to understand that in other families, some parents weren't always good to their kids. Yet the toxicity that sometimes reared its ugly head in competition was offset by the beauty of sportsmanship when good coaches showed us how people are more important than games.

Unfortunately, I learned about aplastic anemia and how tragic some young lives become due to no fault of their own. I realized that strikeouts aren't so terrible when you're awaiting biopsy results. And I discovered how some families must learn everything about a disease they wish they never knew existed.

Of course, there were far more smiles and laughs along the way. The agony of defeat is countered by the thrill of victory, after all. And sometimes, there is even joy in defeat.

One time, after my team got crushed by another team, our sweet coach Butch looked at us all in front of our parents, smiled, and said, "Well, you guys really stunk up the joint."

I was seven years old and feeling a little bad about that until he said, "Now who wants some ice cream?" and in the blink of an eye we were off to enjoy some ice cream as smiling parents placed their arms around our shoulders.

Coach Butch paid for our ice cream, and we devoured our treats alongside the team that creamed us. The resilience of childhood is magical.

The game long called America's "national pastime" is a bit past its prime these days, but few things can pour nostalgia over me like baseball. I've never been much of a poet, but baseball is as close to poetry as I've ever come.

When I put on a glove and catch that first long throw in many months with a loud thump, the muscles in my hands and arms remember. When I smack a pitch into the outfield and sprint from the batter's box, my legs know to swing wide of the line in case there's a chance to make a sharp left turn towards second. And when I hear that crack of the bat connecting with ball, my mind recalls a thousand days beneath a ball cap scolding the sun for blinding me in the face of a high fly ball, then begging that same sun to linger a little while longer so I could have just one more turn at the plate.

Because win or lose, every carefree moment in life is worth more than any diamond.

Clay Morgan is an author, speaker, and business consultant who helps entrepreneurs and professionals overcome communication challenges to connect with others right where they are. Learn more at ClayMorganOnline.com.

Ninth Inning

Marc Gilson

Baseball, A Personal and Biased Perspective

"A hotdog at the ballgame beats roast beef at the Ritz."
~ Humphrey Bogart

I'm not sure just when I became a fan. In truth, I don't think anyone ever chooses to do it. I don't think anyone ever woke up on a Saturday morning and said to themselves, "Today is the day I learn something about baseball." Baseball isn't like that. Baseball, it seems to me, chooses you.

I know this: most of what I learned about baseball is thanks to my dad. And I suspect that most baseball-loving people over the past 100 years would say the same thing. Baseball is like your great-grandfather's pocket watch handed down to you with care. A kind of inheritance, if you will, from your father, grandfather, uncle; often - but not always - a male authority figure.

Baseball fans are a unique breed. While your average baseball fan can discuss the finer points of the game in great detail, the real love the sport engenders in the avid fan is not easy to define. If you spend any time around baseball, it seeps into you in a hard-to-explain way. It's a connecting thread in the linens of one's life. Somehow, game by game, inning by inning, it gets in your blood, and once you've got it there's no cure. Once really exposed to baseball, it will be, for now and always, a wonderful infection, deeply ingrained in your psyche.

If all of this metaphor talk about baseball sounds maudlin or overly-sentimental, you are not a baseball fan. But don't worry, there's still hope for you.

My first exposure to baseball, as I mentioned, was thanks to my dad. Specifically, via the games we would go see played by Portland's minor league team, the Beavers. I suppose I was about eight or nine when I saw my first game. I don't recall the score or who the opposing team was. Maybe surprisingly, I don't even remember whether our beloved Beavers won or lost. Being so new to the game, I didn't understand strikes, balls, outs, steals, or anything else that seemed to be happening in some odd mixture of quiet, deliberate order counterbalanced by sudden, riotous chaos. There were cheers, boos, some running, some dust kicked up, some ball throwing, and even some stealing (when my father said that a runner stole 2nd base, I recall pointing out the obvious: "No he didn't. It's still there.")

I didn't know any of the players, and couldn't tell the catcher from the mascot. I really had no idea what was going on down there on that huge green and brown expanse. I was a baseball newborn, seeing, hearing, smelling the myriad of sensory experiences unique to this bizarre game for the very first time.

I can only recall aspects of the game that really don't have anything to do with sports or statistics.

I will never forget my first sight of the baseball outfield as we entered the stadium, almost blindingly green. I remember the foreign bittersweet smell of beer. I remember the loose crackle of peanut shells under foot. I remember the musky smell of sod and moistened dirt, and of course, the tantalizing scent of hotdogs, and salty popcorn. There is a perfume to a baseball stadium, and it can be found nowhere else. I remember the crack of a 33 ounce bat against a five ounce leathery sphere that sounded like a gunshot echoing in the stadium while the players took batting practice before the game. Most of all, I remember the ever-present noise of the fans, like an ocean, sometimes a quiet drone, sometimes a raucous tidal wave of cheers or boos interspersed with yells of "Get your glasses on, ump!" or, "He's gonna bunt!" or, "Pull that pitcher, he's done!" None of this made any sense to me whatsoever.

Although I was a small boy, experiencing a hundred utterly alien and weird things on that day over 30 years ago, I was overcome with an unexpected feeling - not of being in an uncomfortable and unfamiliar place, but of being at home.

I know that this experience of mine isn't unique. In fact it's almost a cliché. Talk to anyone who loves the game and they will likely have a similar story to tell. But while baseball has not been my life's passion, my appreciation of the Grand Old Game has reached a point with me where I have no choice but to look a little deeper at this odd phenomenon and explore the game in my own way.

> *"I see great things in baseball. It's our game - the American game. It will take our people out-of-doors, fill them with oxygen, give them a larger physical stoicism. Tend to relieve us from being a nervous, dyspeptic set. Repair these losses, and be a blessing to us."*
> ~Walt Whitman

In 1979, the Pittsburgh Pirates, led by Dave Parker and Willie Stargell, won the National League pennant. Anytime I hear their theme song, "We Are Family," by Sister Sledge, I can't help but envision Stargell rounding the bases in his black and yellow Pirate uniform, like some exuberant bumblebee, after one of his famous mammoth home runs.

As it happened, our local minor league team, the Portland Beavers, were the farm team for the Pirates at that time. This resulted in dad and me meeting both Stargell and Parker when they visited Portland during a Beavers exhibition game. Whatever they were like in their personal lives, I remember that Stargell and Parker exhibited all the hallmarks of the gentlemanly demeanor the institution of baseball somehow seems to instill in so many of its stars. And I recall that both of them, while graciously smiling and autographing a nonstop supply of baseballs, seemed to have hands and arms of superheroes, which, in a sense, they really were.

"When they start the game, they don't yell, 'Work ball.'
They say, 'Play ball.'"
~ Willie Stargell

It was then - having met some of its legends - that I began to pay attention to baseball. Although I was already a fan of basketball and football, I found myself constantly mesmerized - if not downright confused - by baseball and its intricacies. That seeming contradiction between simplicity and complexity is but one of the enigmas of the game. Baseball is, after all, unique. Let's remember a few things about baseball that, in my mind anyway, set it apart from other sports.

First, the game is set upon a field arranged in a rather unusual geometric shape. Rather than having a goal of some sort on each end of an elongated field (as most other sports) there is no such goal. No basket, no goal, no net. There is no linear movement from one end zone to the other.

While the specific dimensions and configuration of the lines and bases on the field are constant in major and minor league baseball, the fields themselves can vary in size and shape. The distance from home plate to the center field fence, for example, can vary as much as 35 feet from park to park.

Second, baseball is not a game depending so much on constant action as it is on moments that can unfold in a split second fastball strike, or a single swing that sends a ball over the fence and brings a home crowd to its feet (or leaves them cursing in despair). Once the pitcher fires the ball toward home plate - a journey that takes the ball about half a second - virtually anything can happen. Anything.

Critics of baseball say the game lacks athleticism and hard play. This is a little like complaining that tennis lacks enough slam dunks, or that golf doesn't involve enough tackling. But as anyone who has played or paid close attention to the game can attest, there's plenty of physicality in baseball. The power it takes to smack a ball over a fence 410 feet away may only be eclipsed by the sheer superhuman effort it takes to launch a fist-sized hardball into a space the size of a hubcap sixty feet away...at nearly 100 miles an hour...100 times a night...accurately.

Still, say critics, the game is slow, not enough action to satisfy the short attention spans of the modern sports fan. While the criticism seems misplaced to us baseball fans, do the critics have a point? During an average game, how much time elapses during which "something's happening?"

To get to the bottom of this question, Wall Street Journal reporter David Biderman recently analyzed the amount of time spent in action during an average major league baseball game. "Action," includes the time it takes for a pitcher to throw the ball, as well as the more obvious time a ball is in the air after a hit, or a player is stealing base, etc. Biderman determined that the average game had about 14 minutes of action in it.

However, as noted by Biderman, the time not spent in action during a game isn't exactly time wasted. Between pitches, a myriad of decisions and strategic options may be weighed out. Managers may be busy consulting the hitting chart on an opposing batter before he even steps up to the plate. Catchers and pitchers are having a constant silent dialogue regarding what kind of pitch to throw and where to place that pitch, depending on a range of factors. And fielders may shift positions depending on the batter, or the game situation to increase their chances of saving runs. While the casual observer may grow frustrated by "all the standing around," in baseball, the more involved fan knows that this time spent between pitches is where the real game of baseball is played. In short, there is always "something happening" during a baseball game.

But the critics who persist in impatiently drumming their fingers on their knees and yawning over the "slow pace" of baseball may find it interesting to learn that Biderman also determined the amount of play action during an average professional football game. Just 11 minutes.

While it's interesting to consider these aspects of time where baseball is concerned, most aficionados know that baseball has far more to do with timing. To the novice fan, baseball looks like a sport centered on the pitcher trying to strike out the batter, and the batter trying to avoid such a fate. But to the trained eye, the battle between pitcher and hitter is one of keen decision-making and split-second timing, and it's not a simple thing to analyze. Take pitching, for example.

It would take a supercomputer to properly determine the variables in physics involved in throwing a pitch. From the way a pitcher regulates his breath before the pitch, places his feet on the mound, and adjusts his balance, to the grip on the ball, to the wind-up (often looking like a pained contortionist, but carefully developed by each pitcher to maximize velocity and balance), to the release point (the precise moment the ball leaves the pitcher's hand), and the amount of spin or torque applied to the ball as it is released (the arm swing measured as fast as 5,000 degrees per second!), muscles from neck to toes flexing and releasing, pitching is a perfect symphony of physiological exertion unlike anything seen in other sports.

The speed, movement, and break of a pitch largely determines its success, so the slightest deviant motion or off-balance release can make the difference between a perfectly placed strike or a wild pitch. To master all this, a good baseball pitcher is certainly more than an athlete. He's part physicist, part sleight-of-hand magician, and part gambler.

Batting is no different. A skilled hitter is a combination of laser-like focus, spring-loaded power, and gymnastic balance at the plate. The position and angle of the bat before the pitch is released, as well as the stance, head angle, and knee bend, can be different from hitter to hitter. And then there is the swing itself. There is, as it turns out, a specific way one is supposed to swing at a pitch. Turning the upper body toward the pitcher as the ball is released, rotating the shoulders, and extending the arms only through the strike zone - not before - while following the ball with your eyes, and throwing the entire weight of your hips, arms, and shoulders into the (hopeful) contact. Got it? Good.

Of course not everyone hits this way and keen observers can

recognize some ball players merely by their unique stance at the plate. For an object lesson in contrasts of batting styles among players, observe the differences between Ichiro Suzuki, Alex Rodriguez, Manny Ramirez, Kevin Youkilis, and Alex Pujols at the plate; all outstanding hitters, and yet all possessing radically different batting stances and swings.

Obviously, not everyone cares about such things as whether a hitter is "pulling the ball to left field," or how a pitcher manages to throw a ball in such a way that the trajectory actually changes in mid-flight. As fascinating as these things are to me, I know that the average sports fan probably doesn't spend much time thinking about them. Of course many baseball fans are not "average" sports fans. They may never have held a bat in their hands, but they are students of the game and they devour minuscule pieces of baseball data the way mice gobble crumbs.

> *"Baseball statistics are like a girl in a bikini. They show a lot, but not everything."*
> ~ Toby Harrah

Truthfully, the one element of baseball that was, for a time, off-putting to me is the absolute pervasive worship of The Statistic. Baseball, more than any other sport outside of world economics, maybe, takes statistics very, very seriously. Some have compared the lust for baseball statistics to a drug addiction. It seems that almost nothing can happen during a game - no matter how trivial - that isn't being meticulously documented by somebody somewhere. We've all seen box scores, displaying the runs, hits, and errors, by innings for a given game. Some of us have even looked up things like "lifetime batting average," for a given player, or "best ERA for a closer since 1955." But this does not scratch the surface of statistical obsession with which baseball fans preoccupy themselves.

For example, were you aware that on September 5th, 2006, seven teams shut out their opponents? Or that on July 24th, 2006, the Detroit Tigers became the first team in 115 years to score 5 or more runs in the first inning of three consecutive games? Or that only two brothers ended up with the exact same batting average in the same season (Mike and Bob Garbank, in 1944, a.261 average for both). Still awake?

Well, let me let you in on a little secret: you do not need to concern yourself with such trivia in order to thoroughly and genuinely appreciate the game of baseball. But here's an even deeper secret: the more you watch baseball, the more you will become genuinely fascinated by such seemingly meaningless facts. And you might just learn something in the process. Thanks to baseball, I learned how to calculate a pitchers ERA, a hitter's batting average, and other (gasp!) mathematical feats.

One of the most compelling aspects of baseball to me is that it's really a game within a game, within a game. It's like some sort of fractal image: the closer you look, the more you see. The greater your attention, the more details are revealed. To commit to becoming a student of the game means becoming a kind of archeologist who digs deeper and is rewarded with ever more intriguing information. After more than 30 years of personal appreciation and observation, I am still learning the game. From pitch selection, to situational fielding positions, to the strategy of the batting lineup based on the strengths and weaknesses of the opposing starting pitcher, baseball is a bottomless well of fascination for anyone intrigued by variables, odds, statistics, and just plain luck.

I've rambled on about the ins and outs of baseball for some time now. But what is it about this game that really so grabs me as a fan?

I guess the answer to that runs deeper than hits, home runs, and hotdogs. I think the real answer is that baseball delivers something to my life I've found nowhere else: A sense of belonging. Belonging to a history, a tradition, a heritage that not only stands the test of time, but also makes time somehow irrelevant. Think about it. This game has been played, essentially the same way, since the Industrial Revolution. Through world wars. Through political upheavals. Through social unrest, and times of economic boom and dark depression. It has served as both a focal point and a distraction for numerous generations. It's been a touchstone of American history, both reflecting and deflecting the stresses and influences at work outside the ballpark.

And it's not just an American phenomenon. It's nearly impossible to find a town of more than a few hundred people anywhere on the planet that doesn't include a group of kids swinging a stick at a ball, many with dreams of one day knocking a walk-off homerun out of the park in the bottom of the 9th inning of a World Series game 7. (Hey, I still have that dream too!)

> *"The other sports are just sports. Baseball is a love."*
> ~ Bryant Gumbel

Baseball has it's losers and champions, heroes and goats, its integrity and, yes, its scandals. Like the men who play the game, baseball itself isn't perfect. But somehow, in some mysterious way, baseball inspires, enthralls, and entertains like no other sport.

As for me, I'm grateful dad took me to that first game. I'm happy to have baseball as a part of my life and education. And I've learned more than a few things from baseball over the years. From Babe Ruth, I've learned that the mystique of history can endure into the postmodern age. From Jackie Robinson I've learned that the power of a man's spirit and skill can overwhelm the bitterness of prejudice. From Lou Gehrig I learned that we are all ultimately mortal, and yet all capable of performing superhuman feats. From Derek Jeter I learned that you don't have to be a jerk to win: it's possible to succeed with both style and grace. From Cal Ripkin Jr. who played a staggering record 2,131 consecutive games, I learned the value of resilience, determination, and guts. From Bill Buckner I learned that major league mistakes don't change the fact that life goes on. From Yogi Berra I learned that "Baseball is ninety percent mental, the other half is physical." The list goes on.

A few years ago, my dad and I took my son to his first Portland Beavers baseball game. I don't remember much about the game. I don't recall the opposing team. I don't even recall whether our beloved Beavers won or lost. What I do recall is a great feeling of satisfaction, that I was now able to do what dad had done for me by introducing him to this strange and wonderful world of strikes, steals, and sliders.

Little had changed since my first game. The smell of beer and hotdogs still permeated the air. The field was just as green, the fans just as boisterous, the crack of the bat just as sharp. And, sometime around the 6th inning, sitting there in the stands with my father and son, I recall the distinct and irreplaceable feeling of being at home.

> *"The one constant through all the years, Ray, has been baseball. America has rolled by like an army of steamrollers. It's been erased like a blackboard, rebuilt, and erased again. But baseball has marked the time. This field, this game, is a part of our past, Ray. It reminds us of all that once was good, and it could be again."*
> ~James Earl Jones (as Terrence Mann) in *Field of Dreams*

Extra Innings

Ryan Nowlin

What Baseball Means to Me

Baseball means having fun. Personally, when I play baseball and each time I get a new team, I think...hmmm. This is going to be fun. And I think I am going to get to know each player on the team. It also means making memories with my family and with both my new and old friends.

One season, when I was seven or eight years old I played baseball and my team and another team made it to the championship game. My team lost that championship game, but we still got a trophy for second place. We had a team party to end the season. There were some teammates that were sad because we lost that final game, but there were others that were having lots of fun that night.

Whenever I hear the word baseball, I think of hitting the ball when it's pitched to you and making the last out of the inning and making the game winning catch. My favorite position to play is outer left field. This is because most baseball players are right-handed, so when they hit the ball, the ball usually goes into the left field. It's fun to be the player who catches the game winning out. You don't win every game, but you need to accept that sometimes you win your games and sometimes you lose them. You also need to have good sportsmanship while playing the game or you will be ejected by the umpire.

When I watch baseball, I like cheering on my favorite team, the Los Angeles Angels. I love to watch their games whether it is pre-season, the middle of the regular season, or in the post-season. I am always cheering on the Angel's baseball team players and I also love watching them play during the MLB All-Star Game.

Some basic rules of baseball are, if you hit a pop fly and somebody catches it before the ball hits the ground, fence, or net, you are out. And if you get three strikes, you are out. And if you hit a ground ball to the person in the infield, and they throw it to the first baseman, and if the first baseman catches it before you make it to first plate, you're out.

Baseball also means getting to spend time with my Dad. He used to play baseball when he was a kid and is really good at the game. He coaches me and tells me to only swing at anything that is between my chest and my knees. He also tells me to get closer to the plate. He tells me to bring my lid down and not to swing at it if it isn't a good one. I've learned to take my time and to only swing at good pitches.

I also like to steal bases in between plays. Everything I know about baseball has mostly come from my Dad teaching me. I've learned a little over the years from some of my coaches, but most of what I have learned has been from my Dad.

Editor's Note: Ryan Nowlin is a student and a baseball player living in southern California with his mother, father, younger sister, and younger brother. At twelve years old, Ryan is the youngest of our authors and also the only one who could realistically become a professional baseball player within the next decade.

I had the pleasure of hearing Ryan speak in front of a group of almost a hundred people, young and old alike, and he captivated the audience with his thoughts and insights. At some point in his talk he mentioned that he loved baseball, and that is when I was inspired and prompted to ask him to write about what baseball meant to him so he could be included in this anthology. Ryan represents what is good about our youth, our country, and our future and gives everyone who knows him great hope and promise for what is yet to unfold in the years ahead.

Grand Slam

Dennis Becker

My Love Affair with Baseball

I've been a baseball fan my entire life.

In other words, a long, long time.

And it sort of led me to the career than I now enjoy. Let me explain.

I grew up in northwestern Pennsylvania, one of the first of the baby boomer generation, so that sort of gives you an idea of when I was born.

From about the time I could run, I remember one of my favorite activities was running the bases on a baseball diamond. My family wasn't rich by any stretch of the imagination, in fact quite the opposite, but my Dad, even though he was a huge football fan, knew I was way too small for that sport and made sure I had a glove and bat and ball.

In our small town there were several vacant lots, and my friends and I could always find a place to play, and play we did during the too short summers, from dawn to dark. And even when I couldn't find enough kids to play with, a few of us could always go into our back yard with a Wiffle ball and bat, use imaginary runners, and play that way.

My playing days ended with Little League (age 12) because as much as I loved the game, and as often as I dreamed of being a big league baseball player when I grew up, I had more dreams than athletic ability.

That didn't stop me from idolizing those that did have the talent though, and the closest team to where I lived was the Cleveland Indians.

When I was young, they were actually a pretty good team before their fortunes took a downturn. But as good as they were, the New York Yankees always seemed to be better.

I hated the Yankees, but more on that later.

My favorite players were Herb Score and Rocco (Rocky, "don't knock the rock") Colavito.

Back then, at least in my town, there were very few games on television. There was the Baseball Game of the Week on Saturday, and the World Series. It was a rarity to see my heroes from Cleveland actually play.

Back then, the World Series games were played in the afternoon, and I would sneak my transistor radio into school and listen during class. I don't remember ever getting into trouble, because I think the teachers were actually pretty cool about the whole thing, and they might have had their radios also.

Yes, even when we couldn't watch games on television, there was always radio, and my home town station (WOTR radio in Corry, Pennsylvania) carried Indian games. I remember going to sleep listening to the games with my transistor radio by my pillow.

My mother never had to nag me to go to bed, because that was my favorite place to be after my homework was done, either listening to a game, or listening to rock music radio (usually either WABC radio in New York, or WBZ in Boston, or WCFL in Chicago on clear nights).

My mother was never a baseball fan, but she did have sort of a crush on Mickey Mantle because she thought he was cute.

When the Indians weren't playing at night, I could pick up other teams on a clear night, like KMOX radio in St. Louis, where my favorite National League player, Stan Musial starred.

During my formative years, Sandy Koufax was a phenomenon. His career was cut short because of arthritis, I think it was, but my idol, Herb Score came up to the majors and was destined to be even better...

... until one tragic day when a batter drilled a line drive into his eye. Herb recovered after a while, but was never the same, because his reflexes made him alter his motion to prevent the same thing from happening again. He became a broadcaster for the Indians eventually and had a long career in the game.

So my main hero was Rocky Colavito. Rocky was a great home run hitter. I remember listening to the game when he hit 4 home runs, still a record that he shares with not many others.

I started collecting baseball cards with the money from my 25 cent a week allowance. I can still picture the cards with Herb and Rocky on them in my mind.

Reflecting back, I guess you might say that my Internet marketing career started there, through a few crooked paths, which I'll mention later.

In 1960, the Indians traded Rocky Colavito to the Detroit Tigers for Harvey Kuenn, a good but not great hitter, and the team's fortunes took a quick descent, not to rebound until many decades later. It devastated me.

But I do have great memories of baseball when I was kid.

I remember the first game I went to. My dad was a Boston Red Sox fan, he loved Ted Williams, so he too was a Yankees hater. Cleveland was about two hours away by way of Interstate 90. I still tear up when I remember entering the beautiful (to me) stadium, going through the turnstiles, and finding the way to our seats.

When I first caught sight of the field, it was like heaven. I had never seen grass so green and lush. The scoreboard. The sound of the bat against ball in batting practice. And the game. Unreal. I don't remember who won that game. Probably Boston, but that's OK, I was hooked.

We went to about one game a year back then, and it was always my favorite day of all. Since I grew up, I've gone to my share of games, and remember them all. I remember the first time I took my son to a game. One year we took him and a bunch of his friends to a New York Mets game for his birthday party in May.

Oh, right, the Mets. How did I get to follow the Mets?

In 1977, shortly after getting married, I took a job in New Jersey. I was still an Indian fan, and still listened to many of their games on radio (still very little television coverage where I lived).

When we got to NJ, the good news was that there was plenty of TV coverage of the local teams, but the bad news was that they seldom even mentioned the score of my Indians, and I couldn't pick up the radio stations that carried Indian games.

So being a baseball fan first and foremost, and being a Yankee hater, I had to pick a new team to follow, and that turned out to be the New York Mets.

The Mets weren't very good when I moved here, but as years went by, they got better and actually won the World Series in 1986. My son was coming of age that year, and he latched onto them as his favorite team also. We went to games together, and I remember one very cold, very wet day in October 1988, we went to a playoff game, where the Mets were playing the Los Angeles Dodgers for the NL pennant.

The Mets lost. We froze. But it was a great game and a great time together.

Going back in time, there's one other game that was particularly memorable.

It was June 4, 1974. I was still single, and a friend and I went to the game in Cleveland, against the Texas Rangers. The club was having a promotion, 10-cent beer night, where fans could get a 12-ounce cup of beer for a dime, limit 6 per customer per visit to the concession stand.

The old Cleveland stadium was monstrous, holding about 80,000 fans. That night there was a huge crowd by Indian standards, around 25,000. And the teams hated each other because of earlier incidents between players.

Texas took a lead, which gave the fans more and more reason to ease their pain by getting more beer. Since I was driving home after the game, I only had one or two beers, but many fans made their way to get their 6-cup limit multiple times.

Unbelievably Cleveland came back to tie the game at 5-5 late in the contest.

Eventually the crowd got out of control. Fans ran onto the field, and (you can look this up but you can't make it up) Texas Manager Billy Martin led his team onto the field, wielding bats, because they literally feared for their lives.

It got worse, and the umpires called the game off, the Indians had to forfeit the game.

And of course, that made the fans even angrier. I remember seats being ripped out of the concrete and thrown. It was a riot.

My friend and I quickly left the scene and went back to our car, leaving the crowd to have their "fun".

I don't think there has been a 10-cent beer night there or anywhere else since.

You can read more about the game here:

https://en.wikipedia.org/wiki/Ten_Cent_Beer_Night

Most of the games I've gone to have been relatively uneventful. I still love baseball, but actually now prefer to watch it on television at home, with a comfortable seat and a nearby bathroom and refrigerator. But there's still nothing else like walking to your seat and seeing the lush green grass, hearing the sound of bat on ball, and hoping for a foul ball to come your way.

And no, I never caught a foul ball, but I still hope every time I go to a game.

Oh, I mentioned that path that led me to be an Internet marketer...

Well, I mentioned I collected baseball cards. When I got tired of traveling as a software consultant and trainer, I decided to open up a retail store in my home town, selling... what else?... baseball cards and other collectibles.

And that store eventually led to me selling accessories on eBay, and to setting up a web site, and to learning the ins and outs of marketing online, and to where I am today. A very long story made very short.

And the Yankees which I hated so much when I was a boy and young adult? I'll admit, they're a great team as I write this, with players that I sort of enjoy watching.

But I still follow the Mets and given a chance I still root for the Indians, who have come full circle to be a winning team again.

The more things change, the more they stay the same... I wish the Mets time would come around again.

Post Game

I hope you have enjoyed these writings. The authors are men and women from three countries on two continents and range in age from twelve years old to almost eighty years young. The single thing that connects us all is our mutual love for the sport of baseball, and the people that make this game come to life every season.

This game holds a sacred space in the hearts of so many, and the ball field serves as a microcosm of the most notable events in life and society as a whole. Lessons of friendship, fair play, sportsmanship, and tolerance are everywhere. Team members are worthy of adoration while fans are appreciated for the role they play in the scheme of things.

The next time you are watching a game on television or at the ball park, or discussing the latest plays by your favorite players with your closest friends, think for just a moment about what your life would be like without baseball. Then snap back to reality, knowing that baseball is a constant in the world as we know it and will be around for generations to come. And if you want to know what it truly means to be in love, share baseball with someone special in your life and see firsthand how that feels.

About the Author

Wouldn't take nothing for my journey now.
~ Maya Angelou

Connie Ragen Green is an online marketing strategist, bestselling author, international speaker, and mentor to people on six continents. She is a former classroom teacher, real estate broker, and residential appraiser who left it all behind to start an online business during 2006.

This change of direction with career, lifestyle, and goals occurred as she came to realize that she wanted something more from her life than what she was currently experiencing. This was the beginning of a new life, where anything is possible and everything unfolds in a magical way.

After struggling during her first year of entrepreneurship, Connie finally embraced the struggles of writing and technology, leveled up her work ethic, and continues to exceed her own potential in her life and business.

Making her home in two cities, Santa Barbara, California at the beach and Santa Clarita, California in the desert, Connie is active with a number of charities, non-profits, and service organizations. These include Rotary, an international service organization; Zonta, a women's business organization with the Mission of advancing the status of women worldwide; the Benevolent and Protective Order of Elk; the Boys and Girls Clubs of America; and SEE International, an organization dedicated to restoring the vision of people in many underdeveloped countries.

Becoming an online entrepreneur changed Connie's life forever. Once she became versed in online marketing and observed first-hand how powerful the effect was for people all over the world, she began writing on a variety of topics, creating information products, speaking at live events and workshops, and mentoring people on how to build a successful and lucrative business they can run from home or from anywhere in the world.

Find out more and receive some relevant information right away by visiting https://ConnieRagenGreen.com to further connect with Connie and to begin your own journey of online entrepreneurship.